Hope you'll enjoy redding My book~!

Michael Tanzer

マイケル・タンザー

MICHAELISM

-My POV on Life with Autism-

Author: Michael Tanzer, ASD Advocator

This book is dedicated to those who have autism and are proud....

Keep believing in yourself...

Giving up is for Rookies.... [4]

Go for the Top......

Accept it....

Learn from me....

Be proud of yourself....

To everyone who supported me throughout my life....

Table of Contents

Foreword

I am more than pleased to introduce this wonderful and insightful book by Michael Tanzer. I have had the absolute pleasure and honour of knowing Michael and his family for over 20 years.

I first started working with Michael in the early 1990s when I was an instructional therapist, learning about the principles of Applied Behaviour Analysis and the world of Autism Spectrum Disorder (ASD). His family opened their home to a team of dedicated individuals who were committed to support Michael's learning and growth.

This is Michael's story to tell and I am beyond proud of all his accomplishments over the years. I have been a part of his journey, and can attest to the countless hours his family, therapy team and friends have provided to help Michael reach his potential (and he is not done yet!). He is a young man who has certainly had his fair share of challenges and setbacks, but his dedication and ability to face those fears have been pivotal in his commitment in working towards his dreams.

As a professional who has been in the field for over 20 years, worked with numerous individuals, families, and other professionals, I am constantly trying to build my own educational knowledge. I can honestly say that it has been Michael, who has been teaching me along the way. He continues to amaze me and has helped shaped the professional I have become.

This book is truly an insight into the mind of one young man and what being on the autism Spectrum means for him. To quote Stephen Shore, *"If you have met one person with autism, you have met one person with autism".* Whether you are a parent of a child with ASD, a professional or an individual with ASD yourself, this book shows that even though it can be quite difficult for those diagnosed with ASD, with perseverance, love and support, all individuals can achieve success. When we focus on one's strengths, embrace their challenges and help build self-awareness, success and happiness are possible.

I have genuinely enjoyed reading this book and I am confident that Michael's point of view (POV) will benefit so many. Thank you, Michael Tanzer, for believing in yourself and sharing your story with us.

Janet Arnold
Behaviour Consultant, Public Speaker and Author

www.findingsolutions.ca

Author's Notes

   MICHAELISM: My POV on Life with Autism was written based on my own personal experiences having Autism Spectrum Disorder (ASD). I was diagnosed when I was three years old when I was in Preschool and let me tell you something: it has not been an easy road! I have worked hard with my family and other professionals who have supported me throughout my whole life and continue to help me.

   This book is filled with many different topics that I have a POV (point of view) on. It is about what I think based on my experiences with having autism. I wanted to share my opinions with you while you are reading my book. My POV might be different than your POV and that is okay because everyone has their own opinions based on their own experiences. Everyone with autism is different. This book is NOT intended to provide you with any professional or therapeutic advice. But still, I do hope you learn something about ASD after reading it.

   To be honest with you all, I do hope it helps provide some understanding into the mind of those who have ASD. People with autism should be accepted instead of being thought as different in a negative way. You may find there are some grammar mistakes (and even punctuation mistakes) and that is okay, as this is how I speak. I like to call it, my *MICHAELISM.* Another reason why I call it "MICHAELISM" is because I do not understand a lot of vocabulary and grammar. The English language can be so confusing! So, I hope you can manage to read and understand what I have written and my point that I am trying to tell you. Why edit how the mind of a person with autism thinks? You will also find Japanese expressions throughout the book; this is because it is a language, I taught myself.

   Anyway....I would like to offer special thanks to my loved ones (my family and my relatives), my friends and my therapists. You have helped me make my dreams come true by believing in me and supporting me through this writing process. I would like to give additional thanks to Janet Arnold for helping me with some of the editing and her assistance during this entire writing process.

   I hope you will enjoy reading this book as much as I enjoyed writing it.

Sincerely,

Michael Tarze

ASD Advocator

1 - My POV on Me

So, what do you want to know about me? Well for starters, my name is Michael Tanzer and I started writing

this book during the year of 2018. I have brown hair, hazel eyes, I wear glasses like my parents, and I am an adult with Autism Spectrum Disorder (ASD). I was diagnosed around the age of three. I can be very friendly and will introduce myself when I feel comfortable. I also like to know the names of people, so I always ask. A cool thing about me is that I can write and understand in different foreign languages like Japanese and limited French. I became interested in Japanese culture in high school and taught myself how to read and speak it. I also attended a Japanese community centre to help me learn the language.

My favourite TV show is South Park [1] because I find that show even funnier than Family Guy [2] or The Simpsons [3]. South Park [1] was created by my favourite heroes, Trey Parker, Matt Stone and SEKAI NO OWARI [9]. I hope I will meet them in person one day. I have always loved movies and music and I am PARTICULARLY good at remembering details of the movies I watch. For example, the names of the characters, quotes, the actors from the movie and even dates. Pretty cool, huh? When I was younger, I collected all my favourite movies. Fact: I still have them today. Many people, including those with ASD, like to collect things including video games, movies, and CDs. Basically, anything they may have an interest in or is their hobby. Believe me, I have A LOT of things! Some people may think it is a waste of money, but, I do not. In this book, I am writing about me and my autism. But please remember, I am sharing my experiences and my POV. So basically, how my mind works. If you understand my mind, then maybe you can better understand someone else on the ASD spectrum.

My favourite music genre is J-Pop because it's up-tempo and more energetic than typical American music and my favourite artists have to be SEKAI NO OWARI (Pronunciation: SE-K-EYE NO OH-WAR-EE) [9], NAOTO INTI RAYMI [10], EXILE [11], MISIA [12], J Soul Brothers III from EXILE TRIBE [13], m-flo [14], KODA KUMI [15], ayumi hamasaki [16] and Utada Hikaru [17]. Do you know any of them? If you are a J-Pop fan, then yes you do know them. Back in 2004 when I was in Grade 7, I first discovered J-Pop when I was watching an Utada Hikaru [17] music video on my laptop. I just loved it so much. I became interested in this music. Some people say that people with autism who have a special interest in something can be obsessive. Well, for me I think that is a negative term. I mean, we ALL have things that we are interested in and if you love it, and you spend time doing it, you learn from it. So how is that bad? Right? Look, I have an interest in Japanese culture and I taught myself how to speak and write it. 100% true! Technically, I also want to meet SEKAI

NO OWARI[9] in person one day. That is not being obsessed. Isn't there someone you would love to meet one day? True: I did like to spend a lot of time doing the things I was super interested in and I did need reminders to try or do other things. I think we need to encourage people with autism to try different things to get them feeling more comfortable and hopefully build their interests so they can learn new skills. Especially if we are trying to help them get a job one day. This is important. I may have tried to argue at first, but now I have way more interests. My point is, interests are important, and we all have them. We can learn new skills by being able to experience the things we love.

I am also what some people may call an overly sensitive person. What does this mean? For me it means that there are a lot of different things that bother ALL my senses and feelings. A term I heard to label this was called "hyper" or "hypo" sensitive. This means I either seek or avoid different things because of my senses. Things like smells, sounds, tastes, and touches. For example, going to a restaurant used to be EXTREMELY hard for me. There were so many disgusting smells that seriously bothered my nose, and so many loud noises that hurt my ears. My parents always encouraged me to go to new restaurants (I loved McDonald's), to try new foods (not just French fries and chicken nuggets), and over time I started to like more foods. Now I eat much better and can go into ANY restaurant at anytime even with short notice. Amazing, right? I have learned to love many new foods except I still do not like salads or some vegetables. For me it is about the smell of those things and okay, the taste too. The smells make me feel sick. Although, I will eat veggies in soups. Strange. My family is encouraging me to take cooking lessons. I am not so sure about that; but I may try.

You might be wondering what happened when I was younger with all these sensory issues? Well, I refused (I mean yelled and screamed and dropped to the floor). When I had to go into a restaurant, except for McDonald's, I only wanted to order certain foods (only the ones I liked) and one type of drink. But doesn't everyone? Since it was a long time ago, I do not remember everything, but I do know my family never gave up. When I was little, I only ate a few foods so that made it extremely hard for everyone, especially me. How was it hard for me? For starters, the way it impacted my senses, and then all those meltdowns. Having a meltdown is not easy for parents and it is also hard on a kid too! It can be so exhausting and confusing. As an adult, I still order what I like but I like a lot more foods now. My favourite drinks are Diet Pepsi[5] and Diet Coke[6]. Over the years, my therapists and my parents would take me to different restaurants until I became comfortable. Being open to new restaurants is great. I can visit other countries and go into a new restaurant easier now. This is a huge accomplishment that many people who have autism or know someone who has it can understand. Am I right? You get it!

So, how did I accomplish all of this? When my family and therapists took me to new restaurants. Sometimes, we did not even order food. We just sat and practiced being in a new place with all the different sounds and smells. Oh yeah, I also tried new foods at home first. For example, we ordered take-out from a new restaurant and practiced having it on my plate and smelling it (Blagh!). The first step was just getting used to looking at it and smelling the food. I did not even have to eat it! Thank goodness! Later, when I was comfortable with looking at it and smelling it, I had to lick it, then eventually chew it, and then swallow it. You get the picture! Do not get mad at me, but my POV is that I do not think parents do this enough with their kids. I mean you must help them. It is not going to be easy, but I know they can do it. Just like me! I also did a food course at school and it did help me a lot. I try to overcome this food issue everyday. The more I think about it and write about my experiences, I DO think cooking courses will be a good thing for me. Maybe I will start small. I can watch cooking videos first and then do a course.

I am also sensitive about laughter. I think I have a particularly good sense of humor and understand sarcasm and jokes on TV shows and movies. However, sometimes after I say something, and someone starts to laugh I feel anxious. I am not always sure if they are laughing at me (in a mean way) or at what I said. I know I should ask them what they are laughing at, but it happens so quickly. , Then I feel unsure of myself and usually end up saying *"Stop laughing at me"* and then I might ask why they are laughing. It can be so confusing because I never laugh at anyone. I only laugh at fictional stuff like movies and TV shows. My POV is if you laugh at what someone who has ASD just said, try to smile and say, "Don't worry, I am not laughing at you". You might have to do this many times before they understand and do not get upset. Just remember, it can be hard to look at your face, listen to you and understand what you are saying all at the same time! Confusing, right?!

Let us talk about clothing. Have you ever seen someone with ASD who wears the same thing repeatedly? Please do not assume that they are not changing their clothes. My POV is that they have a lot of the same clothes because they feel good on their skin. Take me for example, sometimes I will wear blue jeans, but I prefer to wear track pants instead. I think everyone agrees that they are way more comfortable! To be honest, I do not really remember the last time I wore jeans. (They probably do not even fit me anymore.) Jeans and other pants feel too tight on my legs and around my waist. Also, I really do not like the feeling of the buttons on my shirts against my skin. It feels uncomfortable. Like something is poking at me. So, I own a lot of loose T-shirts. I hope I never have to wear a tuxedo one day!

Everyone has talents, even people with ASD. My talents are being able to type with super speed, learning to speak different languages (like Japanese and some French) and knowing a lot about movies. These are all things I could do at an early age and taught myself. Pretty cool eh? (I may have forgotten to mention that I am Canadian, and we sometimes end our sentences with "eh?"). One thing many people do not know is that when I was little, I could not speak. Many kids with autism cannot speak when they are young. So, my family tried to use pictures with words to help me communicate. In the end, I learned how to read before I could speak in full sentences. I read before I could speak and now, I am writing a book. I have also written a few articles for an autism magazine called autism Matters. Everyone has talents, so do not give up looking for them. It might surprise you what they can do. Hopefully, their talent will help them later in life, like for a job.

Did I mention that I have good hearing? I can hear things from a distance. Sometimes my parents would have a conversation downstairs and I am in my room with the door closed, with the fan running, TV on and I can still hear them talking and know what they are saying. However, some sounds bother me. When anything has a volume up full blast, that really hurts my ears. My POV is that life can be a real challenge when you have ALL these sensory issues. Please try to be patient and more understanding. We are not trying to be difficult. This is very real for many people on the spectrum.

I will say this…

I know I have talents, but some things are still hard for me, like money management and dealing with my anxiety. Though they might be hard, I still want to learn how to deal with both issues. You will learn more about me and my POV on autism as you read this book. Just give me a chance!

So please, get to know me.

どうか、僕を知ってください。

(Dou ka, Boku wo shitte kudasai)

Chapter Summary POV

- o Having a special interest should NOT be called an obsession. It does not have to be a negative thing.

- o We ALL have things we are interested in and if you love it, spend time doing it, and you learn from it, it is not a good thing.

- o Everyone has talents. Even people with ASD.

---

2 - My POV on Autism Spectrum Disorder

I believe there a lot of things that you should know about what having Autism Spectrum Disorder means for me. I am not here to tell you what having autism is like in general because everyone is different and so is their experience. For me, I think having autism is a blessing and I am lucky to have it. I must admit that I did not always think this especially if I am having a really hard day. When I found out about my autism (I cannot remember at what age), my therapists and family had to help me understand what it meant. It was a foreign word. It was a word I had overheard my parents say before, but I never understood what it looked like or sounded like. I mean, when my therapists were teaching me how to speak and understand language, a picture of a car or a toy car with the label car was easy to learn and understand. It was a clear example of something concrete. But, this word, AUTISM-No clue!

It took a long time (and patience) to really understand this term as it applies to me. There was a time when I thought it meant I was stupid or not good enough and that I was different in a negative way. To be honest with you, sometimes I used it as an excuse when things got too hard. So, you cannot use this label as an excuse because it is very rude, unfair and it is not right for me or anyone. This thought still pops into my head, but I try to fight it away. But the thing is that accepting my autism took a while. It meant having a lot of conversations with my family, teachers, and therapists. They never gave up on me. I believe that you need to tell someone about their ASD. You should do it in a way that they can better understand and be proud of who they are. We can only accept it when we understand what it means.

I sort of understand why you might be afraid to tell your children that they have autism. Are you afraid they will not understand? Are you worried that they would think bad about themselves? Are you ashamed? Are you scared what others will think about them or how they will treat them? Well, if you do not tell them and they hear someone else say it, they might think it is a bad thing. This was my truth! The point is, I am very smart when it comes to things like this. Having autism made me who I am. For example, not only did I teach myself different languages, but I am also a fast typer (I know I mentioned this before-just in case your forgot). I also taught myself how to read. Oh yeah, I am writing a book. Rather good for someone on the spectrum! Do you know someone with autism? What are the things that they are great at? Do they know? Did you tell them? If no, why not? What do they feel proud about?

Having autism does not make me stupid, but instead it makes me special. It makes me the way I am. You may not understand everything that I am saying or writing, but for me, I call it MICHAELISM ("my Autistic English"). It is how I speak and understand what is going on. Again, this is my truth. I have challenges because of my autism, but I am learning to accept them, and so should you. I will discuss this later in other chapters.

Many people think that people with ASD do not want friends, but this is **NOT** true. I wanted friends and I made friends; some are on the spectrum and some are not. I have great friends that I have known for a long time. All my friends share the same interests with me. It was a little bit hard to make friends, but I got support from my family and my therapy team.

Although autism may make me a little different, I am still important, unique, and special. Some people focus on the label and might say, *"I am an autistic person"* or *"A person with autism"* but to be honest, I prefer *"I am Michael."* Yes, it is true that I have autism, but I also have dark brown hair, light skin, and wear glasses. Why do we need to use the label to identify a person? I guess in some situations it is important that some people know (for example in school). But I do not go around telling strangers at the store, *"Hey, I have Autism and my name is Michael"*. Or a fictional character would say on TV: *"I'm Scott Malkinson and I have diabetes"*[1]. It is true, you should not hide who you are or be ashamed, but YOU have the right to tell who you want to tell. Sorry if you disagree. This is my POV remember. This is my story, and these are my thoughts that I want to share with all of you. I was born to love everyone instead of hating each other.

My POV, when it comes to having a disability, is that it not only helped me, but it can help others understand and overcome some of their challenges. I am happy with the way I am. And so, should you! Someday, I hope I will be noticed for my generous personality and earn a chance to be accepted by the whole world. This is my gift...my destiny....and my path to accepting my autism.

Chapter Summary POV

- Do not be afraid to tell your child that they have Autism Spectrum Disorder

- People with autism DO want friends

- Be PROUD of who you are!

3 - My POV on Accomplishments

I thought this would be an easy chapter to write but I was wrong. When I start typing my mind thinks of things that I failed at or the things that I think I failed at. The thing is, I am talented! People with autism do have many accomplishments. I know I do! If I try hard to think about it and talk with my family and therapists, I can think of many things I have accomplished in my life. Growing up I had to learn and try everything the other kids were learning. Sometimes it took me longer, but I did it in the end. Like bowling, swimming, skating, bicycle riding and roller blading. After I learned something, then I could decide if I liked it enough to continue.

A huge accomplishment was teaching myself to read when I was four years old. YES, you read that right. I taught myself how to read! Even though I could not talk when I was little, I was always interested in books, newspapers, and magazines. My family read to me and put labels up all around the house. This helped me to become interested in words. I really wanted to know what the words meant. I could sort of see the words with pictures in my head and remember what it said. I have heard people say that someone with ASD is a visual learner. I guess this means I learn better with pictures. It is true! Well, for me anyway (maybe not someone you know with autism). Even today, I prefer to have things written down to help me understand better or help me calm down when I feel anxious.

Another accomplishment was graduating from high school. I feel like I should have dropped out of high school. But fortunately, I did not. My parents and therapists believed in me and helped me with my schoolwork. Let us be honest, school was HARD. This was true for me! I needed support my entire school life. My parents had to fight to have extra help in my classrooms. I mean, really? WHY? In my opinion, schools should help kids who are on the spectrum more. I know things have changed since I was in school, but I think it could still be better., you know. Maybe they can have these people volunteer in schools or give workshops to help train educators.

Speaking of chances, a huge accomplishment that most people cannot say that they have done was to learn to speak and write new languages. In elementary school, I took French and even though it was sort of hard, I never gave up. I have also taught myself to read, write and understand Japanese. I did this when I was in high school. To teach myself, I watched Japanese music videos and clips from various variety shows on the internet. I also went to a Japanese culture program. Now, how many people can say that they taught themselves a new language? Well I did! People with autism have things they are EXTREMELY interested in. My POV is to let them do it! Let them talk about it, watch it, explore it. I mean EVERYTHING okay! If my family stopped me from my interests, I would NOT speak Japanese!

これは Reality でしょう?

(Kore wa Reality deshou? / Is this Reality?)

I also taught myself how to type very quickly on the keyboard by staying on the computer every day from an early age. Thankfully, my school allowed me to use a computer to do most of my schoolwork. I am sure I can type faster than anyone else. I can type without looking at my keyboard with little typing errors. I hope this helps me later with a job. I still want to learn other computer skills. I am good with Microsoft Word, PowerPoint but I do keep having trouble learning the Microsoft Excel program. I think it is because of math (which I will write about later), so stay tuned!

I am also proud (and so is my family) that I have written a couple of articles for the magazine autism Matters which is a publication of autism Ontario. At first, I felt nervous and was not sure they would accept my article, but I sent it anyway. And they did accept it. I am trying to be an ASD advocator and trying to change people's views on autism. This is one reason why I decided to write this book. I want to gain attention and acceptance for people on the spectrum. If you accept me for having autism, then you should accept other people for having autism. You should accept everyone for who they are. People are born with ASD, so it is not their fault.

Finally, my last accomplishment is that I am writing this book and it is helping me gain acceptance and happiness. I hope to become a successful ASD advocator or maybe I would rather be a multi-media producer instead. Or who knows, maybe both right? As I accomplish new things, I might change my mind. To be honest with you, I really want acceptance. I do not want to be treated like I am different.

Everyone has accomplishments every day and we must celebrate even the small things in life. These lead to bigger things, this is true for me. My mom has been good at keeping a record of all my things since I was young. For example, things like certificates, report cards, and other things she and my dad were proud of my whole life. You should do this too so you can be proud of yourself every day! That is the main reason of course. Always be proud of yourself and people on the spectrum.

Chapter Summary POV

- People with autism DO have many accomplishments.
- More support is needed in schools to help people with ASD
- We must celebrate even the small things in life.

4 - My POV on School

Let us face it, school can be hard for any kid, especially a kid who is diagnosed with autism. As I grew up, I attended four different schools where thankfully I made friends. Some of these friends are still my good, long-time friends now. Pretty cool, isn't it?

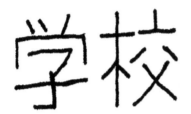

Some people think it is not possible,

でも見てよ！やったね。

(But look! I did it. / Demo mite yo! Yatte ne)

What was the best part of school? Well, it was Grade 8---it was going to Ottawa on a school trip with my friends. I am sure my parents and teachers did not think I would ever be able to go on a school trip by myself when I was young. Well, they were wrong. This was the first time in my entire life that I did not have a helper with me! I hope every kid gets a chance to go on a school trip, even if it is a small one. My experience was great, and I will remember it for my entire life.

I attended high school from 2006 to 2011. It was a tough experience sometimes for me. During my high school years, I learned a lot of what it feels like to be a real "high Schooler". What was painful, you ask? First, it was some of the subjects, like MATH, Learning Strategies and English. Some kids were friendly and some of them were very rude. I do not recall getting physically bullied but what they said was hurtful. No one ever said anything to my face, but I would hear what they said in the hallway or see them laughing at me. To be honest, I do not recall exactly what they said, but I know it was wrong. It always gave me an uncomfortable feeling. Just because it seems like someone does not understand, or is different from you, it does not mean they do not hear you or that they do not understand. I feel lucky that no one ever bullied me to my face at school. I hear about that all the time and it makes me mad. I mean, we are all different and that is okay. We need to teach other kids not to pick on someone with autism just because they are different, or anyone who they think is "different." This is the reason why I want to be an ASD advocator. Just do not be a bully to people with autism or anyone else. Accept people for who they are. I know that some people believe that people on the spectrum cannot read faces or expressions. This is not always true. At first, it was hard for me but then I understood, and I knew when someone was being unkind.

I always had a helper at school, even high school. Sometimes the school had the helper and sometimes my parents had to pay extra for the helper. Crazy right? My POV is that schools should pay for the helper NOT the parents. I mean, families who have kids with autism already must pay for so much. In Canada, the government gives schools money for kids with ASD, but my POV is, it is still not enough because these kids need a lot of help. Kids with autism have the right to be in school and should be in school because they CAN learn. You just must teach them in a way that they can learn.

Come to think of it, school was tough for a while because I had a hard time making new friends. It was not easy. My parents set up lots of play dates when I was little. This was so important, and I think all parents who have kids with autism need to do this. I met kids who were in the same class and our parents arranged visits. We went to the movies, bowling, swimming and did other things in the community. I still meet once a week with some of these people.

Another hard part of attending school was learning English. The thing about English is that it was and still is very confusing for me. I keep a journal that has new words and new meanings that I can learn every day whenever I want. I always had people helping me at school with my homework, this included my teachers, my teaching assistants and of course, private teaching shadows (helpers). *"Wow that was a lot of help!"* but in the end, it DID work out good for me. Why you ask? Because I am writing a book. I know it might be hard to always follow what I am saying. But remember, it is my MICHAELISM after all.

One of the worst subjects at school for me had to be Math. The reason why I do not like Math is because it is so confusing (more than English) and crazy <u>HARD</u>! It does not always make sense to me (especially word problems-remember English?) My therapists tried teaching me about money and adding and subtracting. To be honest I just prefer to use a calculator. As an adult with autism, my family helps me with my banking, but I am happy to say I have my own bank card. This is way easier than using cash. I think this is just one of those skills that I will always need help with.

I guess I should write about something positive about school. Well, one great thing about school was the work experience programs. I will talk more about it in the volunteering chapter. But I will say this, all kids need the chance to do this. Work experience helps get people out of their shell, meet new people, and learn new skills so they can get a job one day. I needed a helper with me when I did my work experience but that is okay. I learned valuable skills and built up my confidence.

I think it is too late for me to attend college or university now (your POV might be different). The thought of going to school causes me anxiety, and I do not want to have a helper with me. So instead, I would prefer to take online courses like Computers, Money, Music, Technology, Film or Photography. My family disagrees, but the important thing is that I still want to learn, right?

Even though I thought school was hard, I did not fail. I passed high school and I got surprisingly good grades. Gotta say, I have survived school throughout the ages. So, if I can, so can you! Stick with it, be positive and you will not fail.

Chapter Summary POV

- o School can be a difficult place for people with autism, but it does not have to be!

- o Every person should get the chance to go on a school trip.

- o Just because it seems like someone does not understand, or is different from you, it does not mean they do not hear you or that they do not understand.

- o More support should be given to kids in school. Kids with autism should be in school because they CAN learn.

- o All kids will benefit from work experience programs

5 - My POV on Anxiety

I have been dealing with anxiety for as long as I could remember. Some of the things that got me upset in the past and still do today are: changes in routine, being corrected (or being criticized), power outages, loss of a relative, loud noises, being ignored, isolated, and feeling left out in real life. I know some of these seem like little issues to you (well of course not the loss of a relative), but they feel big to me when they happen. They cause me stress. Don't you have little things happen to you that stress you out? I am not sure how they got started. Somethings do not bother me anymore; new ones pop up and others disappear. It is strange?

One thing that has been with me my whole life and causes me anxiety and makes me feel nervous is when I hear elephant sounds or see them. I must plug my ears and hum until they go away, or the sound stops. This I have had since I can remember and do not know if I will ever overcome it. When I was young, I LOVED all the Disney movies and owned a copy of all of them. If I am at a movie theatre and I see an elephant on screen I may start to hum. I have learned not to hum too loud but please if you are around, do not stop me from doing it, OKAY. You may know people who do some self-stimming. Before you try to stop it, try to figure out WHY they are doing it. Maybe they are feeling anxious and it helps them. I know it sometimes helps me. I will talk more about this later in a chapter on self-stimming.

Another example of when my anxiety increases is whenever company comes to town. (I mean when they stay at my house), I feel anxious all the time because the routine changes. I like many things to be the same. In the end I manage, but I always have a feeling of uneasiness. My therapists and my teachers have helped me over the years in dealing with changes. There are still some things that I prefer not to change. I cannot always explain why I do not like changes. I guess I just understand the world better when things are the same. Another thing that makes me feel anxious and frustrated is whenever I get criticized by others. I am sure they are not really criticizing me, maybe just giving me their feedback, but it feels like it. Who knows, right? My point is, I cannot keep on having anxiety issues every day because it is not good for me. The real question is, how am I going to overcome my anxiety? I am still trying to figure that out.

When I am feeling anxious, I feel like quitting, yelling, or going to my room and staying there. What helps me is to text a person who makes me feel safe rather than doing these things or posting my feelings on social media (this is such a bad idea). I text the person what I am feeling, and what made me upset. Sometimes this even helps me to remember to ask myself how I can calm down on my own. Even though I want to give up, safe person coaches me not to give up or to try to let things go. Depending on the situation it may take awhile for me to calm down, but in the end, I always do. Giving up is NOT an option at all because you cannot do that and that is not good for you.

It is easier for me to share my feelings through text because talking seems to be a lot harder when I am feeling anxious. It also helps for me to go to my room which is also a safe place. My advice to you is to help your children (or yourself) identify a safe person and a safe place that they can go to every time they are, or you are upset. Listening to music also helps me a lot before. Why not try to follow my footsteps? Other things that work are giving me choices (write them down please!), talk less (this is important because I cannot really hear you when I am super stressed) and oh yeah, be patient. ALWAYS!

So, what do I sound and look like when I am anxious? Whenever I am upset, I might raise my voice, swear, pace, blame others, and question myself. Those are the five things that I always do when I am upset. Do not be afraid to question yourself. Feeling anxious is okay if you find helpful ways to calm yourself down and feel good again. I personally try to let things go whenever it is too hard especially whenever I am out in public. I had to learn this. Other people should be taught to do the same. It will take time, but it can be done.

I worry a lot about things that might happen and when I worry, I might yell. This causes confusion for a lot of people. But guess what, it causes confusion for me too. I remember when I was little, I got anxious at the mall when I was with my therapist. Everything was so loud! It was a mall I had never been to before and there were a lot of people and noise. I dropped to the ground and started screaming. My therapist, Janet tried to help, and I started yelling, *"Stop! Help! You are kidnapping me!"* Of course, she was not kidnapping me. I was just filled with so much anxiety. Thankfully, no one called the police on her. The point is a life filled with anxiety is not a life anyone wants to live.

Sometimes my anxiety is way too big. People have different POV's on taking medication to help. Well, for me it does help. I am not telling you to take anything of course. I just want you to know that I do. Finding the right medication can be hard. My parents took me to see many different doctors to help me find the right medication and amount. It did take a long time to find the right medication for me.

A current example of my anxiety was writing this book. It has not been easy for me. I often thought, *"I am going to have to give up on this book."* or *"This book is going to be a flop."* It is bringing back a lot of painful unpleasant memories and there are many times that I wanted to give up writing. I would even rant. I was afraid that people were going to think, *"Who the hell is Michael Tanzer?"*, *"Why should I care?"* or *"Who would want to buy this book?"*

These thoughts really made me upset at times. There were some days that this would make me have a panic attack and stop me from wanting to write. But I did not. My coach and long-time friend, Janet would help me overcome my anxiety. She helped me remember why I wanted to write this book in the first place. It has taken a long time to write this book and there were many edits, but in the end, I did not give up.

So, do not freak out or overreact...because those are NOT options at all. You cannot just be negative every day. Try hard to be positive. Like how I am trying to be. Let go of your bad days and focus on the positive ones. Having positive days is the only way for us to move ahead. You cannot give up that easily. Take things one step at a time and focus on the positive side of you.

Chapter Summary POV

- Many people with autism live with anxiety daily.

- You may know someone who does some self-stimming. Before you try to stop the stimming, try to figure out WHY they are doing it.

- Make sure the person with autism has a safe person they trust.

- Never give up!

---

6 - My POV on Emotions

Some people think that people with autism do not experience complex emotions...they are wrong! I feel anger, sadness, happiness, disgust, jealousy, empathy, love, and anxiety (as well as many more). The question is: How do I show these emotions to others? It is true that some  people with autism show their emotions differently. When I am angry, you know it because I raise my voice and I sometimes swear, though I try not to. I show being happy by smiling and laughing. Sometimes I even feel the need to hug or put my hands on the shoulders of a friend or a family member. If I do this to you, do not be afraid. This just means I am happy. Do not be alarmed, I would NEVER do this to a stranger. Also, I would never hit when I am mad. I never want to hurt others. Yes, I might want to punch my pillow or think about throwing a pop can (only if I  am drinking one), but I will not hurt anyone at all, not ever! I may even try to keep on arguing with someone when I am upset too. It is just that I feel these emotions so strongly and sometimes it might take me a bit longer to calm down, especially if I am having a panic attack. When I am upset, I HATE hearing when people tell me to calm down. I know I must calm down and I do try, honest! I have gotten much better at calming down. My coach, Janet, has told me it is like a pot of boiling water. Sometimes your pot is small and boils faster, and sometimes a larger pot can take longer to boil and to cool down. The important thing is to try and not get discouraged

When I was younger it helped when my therapists or family members wrote down what I needed to do. To be honest this still does help me a lot. Yes, I did tear up the paper sometimes or scratch out the words and write what I wanted. For example, *"Yes yelling helps me!"* My therapist would just get a new piece of paper and write that she wants to help and would give me choices. Sometimes I wanted a different choice, like staying mad, but when I read the words over again, it helped to calm me down. It was like a light switch being turned on or off. So, if you can write down or show a picture to someone of what they need to do, it could help them to calm down. I bet it will help them. Remember, it takes time and a lot of practice.

Once I made a better choice, I would start to feel calmer. I would even apologize to the person because I felt bad afterwards and I did not want (and still do not want) anyone to be upset with me. On a negative note, you should know that I have had a few seizures in the past because of the panic attacks and because of being so upset. I do not really know what is happening when I am having one. My family tells me that I stop talking, make a sound and lie down on the ground. After a panic attack, I am tired, and I want to sleep for a long time.

When it comes to happiness or joy, I like things that are humorous. I may not laugh at the same things that the other people laugh at, but that is okay. For example, I love laughing at South Park and various video clips on YouTube. Sometimes it is hard to recognize what feeling I am having when something causes me so much stress for me. Being happy is easier than being negative every day, don't you agree? I think if your child is having a hard time communicating all their emotions, you should try making a feelings dictionary. This is a dictionary that has faces, descriptions and examples that might describe certain feelings.

I know I don't always show it, or it takes me a long time to show it, but I do show others that I feel sad or bad for what I may have done or said to them. After feeling angry or scared and I calmed down, I tell the people that I am sorry by holding their hands or running my hand on their arms. Then I tell them that I am sorry and ask them if they forgive me. When I was younger, I would write an apology letter. I do not like it when someone is unhappy with me. But who does, right?

Pressure or touch can help me to calm down when I am upset. But still only when I am ready for it. When I was little, I remember screaming a lot at my parents, my teachers, and my therapists when I did not like what was happening. I have learned to speak calmer and tell them how I felt. I also liked to write it down. Come to think of it, I still do write it down. When I am feeling stressed, I will text my family members or my therapists. This really helps me. I think the MOST important thing to teach someone with autism is that they must learn how to express their feelings in an acceptable way.

I am not so sure, but I do think that feeling love is the hardest for me. Again, I know I feel love, and I want others to be happy and not mad at me. I love my family and my relatives of course and I do hope to find love one day with a partner. I am not positively sure if I can get married or not, but time will tell.

Chapter Summary POV

- We do feel emotions! Some people with autism show their emotions differently.

- EVERYONE should learn how to express their feelings in an acceptable way.

7- My POV on Friends

Many people might think that people with autism do not want friends. But this is 100% not true. Why do people think that? Did someone tell you this? Are you guessing? I DO want friends! Sometimes it can be harder than I thought. If someone said they do not want friends maybe it is because they had a bad  experience, or they are afraid, or they are not sure how to make a friend. I mean there could be thousands of reasons why. During my school experience, I have made lots of friends (some who do not have ASD and some who do). I am happy to say even as a young adult, some of the kids I met in high school are still my good friends today.

The truth is: I am not alone.

真実は、一人じゃないよ。

(Shinjitsu wa, Hitori janai yo)

I am glad I met new friends who shared the same interests as me. It does not really matter if they are on the spectrum or not. I am glad I have friends who are cheerful, polite, energetic, funny, and kind-hearted. In the end, I know they got my back. Even if there is physical distance, they will always be in my heart. I have learned a lot of ways to improve my friendships with everyone. They have shown me the truth about the meaning of true friendship. The more people I meet, and the more friendships I make, the more I will bloom into a better and stronger friend than I was before.

From a young age, I always had friends who looked out for me, especially in school. I remember a girl who was a true kind friend. She would help me during class and play with me at recess. Even though it took years for me to talk, she was kind and always knew what I wanted. I know it can be frustrating not understanding what a person with autism wants but guess what, it is frustrating for that person too! We need more kids like this girl in school. Parents and teachers should help teach other kids about ASD and how to be more friendly. Everyone focuses on the kid on the spectrum all the time. True, some people need more teaching about different social skills, but what about the other children? They need teaching about how to be a good friend to people on the spectrum. There are a lot of books and videos to help teach kids all of this. In the end, we need to teach everyone how to just be kind!

So, how did I make some great friends? My parents helped me make friends. They always arranged playdates with kids from my class or my neighborhood when I was young. Sometimes my therapist would be there for me to help with the playdate. These playdates helped teach me how to feel comfortable around kids my age and they helped teach them to feel good about me. It was a win-win situation. Most of the playdates were at my house until I felt comfortable and then we would go out to the community (like a park, play place) and then to their house. My therapists even brought kids they know (their own children, other clients, etc.) to help work on my social skills. When I was growing up there were not very many (maybe not even at all), social skills groups like there are now a days. My family had to rely on kids from school, my community, and summer camps.

One thing we must remember is that every school probably has a child with ASD, so all kids need to feel okay around people on the spectrum. All kids should learn how to be a good friend to everyone. Do not be afraid, okay.

Just do not be afraid of yourself! (My Michaelism for believing in yourself)

君は、自分を恐れないね。

(Kimi wa, Jibun wo osorenai ne)

The more comfortable I became with playdates, the more I started to talk to them. Talking more helped me play better too! Something what I loved doing was playing with trains, building Lego, and going to the park. It was a bit hard playing with the things other kids liked, especially if it was not what I liked doing. I remember sometimes wanting to go be by myself. You need to let kids do this (even if it is for a couple of minutes). Every person needs a break because it can be too much, and they might feel overwhelmed. Do not get mad at them or force them okay. Just start small. Instead of a two-hour playdate why not try 30 minutes and then go up to a longer time. Baby steps! If it does not work, then you can always try again later. Do not give up!

Play dates can be hard. Sometimes there is too much talking, laughing or other loud noises that I did not like. The hardest thing for me (and still sometimes now) was when kids say one thing, but their faces did not match. Confusing right?! (This is still hard for me now). I know they say people on the spectrum have poor eye contact, but this is not always true. I look at the eyes of people but what confuses me is when they laugh at something that I think is not funny. Sarcasm and jokes are hard for me. I prefer when my friends not use that language. Even to this day, I am still learning the meaning of different phrases.

When I was in high school, my parents signed me up for a social skills group in our area. It was okay! It did help a bit. At first, I did not want to go. I felt anxious about it. To be honest, I usually feel anxious about starting something new. Sometimes I am afraid people will not accept me, will laugh at me, or just not like me. I also do not like disappointing anyone. When I start something new, I always think it will be hard. After a few times of going, I feel a lot better. The good news was that some of my friends were in the group too. Even as an adult my mom signed me up for different adult programs at a place for people with ASD to meet new people and learn new skills. I think this is so important.

I think some people, kids or even adults do not want to go to different programs because they are not sure if it will be a good match. I often hear people using the terms "high" or "low" functioning to describe people with ASD. I do not like these terms because it can really hurt their feelings. So instead of judging who is in the program just give it a chance and get to know the people.

When I am volunteering, I meet lots of new people and it is a good place for me to practice my social skills with others. I do not want to give up and hope to find a paying job where I can make new friends. I still want more friends. I am happy that I still see some of my old friends from high school every Thursday. It is pretty cool!

Why not follow my footsteps to make new friends?

Chapter Summary POV

- People with ASD do want friends.
- You might have to help people with autism learn how to make friends and help other people learn how to be friends with someone with ASD.
- Setting up play dates can help all kids learn how to be better friends.
- Try different programs where you can meet new people.

8- My POV on Hobbies

Many people with ASD have hobbies. Sometimes people say that these hobbies are obsessions. I do not like when I hear people say that it is an "obsession". Yes, it is a special interest, but when I hear non-autistic people say it, it sounds like it is a bad thing. Having hobbies are normal for everyone! If people spend a lot of time doing one thing, they get really good at doing it. Maybe you must ask why it looks like an obsession. Hobbies are especially important to me. I like drawing, tracing, sketching pictures on traditional or digital paper, photography, photoshop, and the newly founded talent of writing. You will see some of my artwork in this book. I have been inspired by many people. I hope you like my drawings.

My hobbies help me when I feel like I am bored or have nothing to do. Keeping busy is a good thing for a lot of people, even those who are on the spectrum. Whenever I am doing one of my hobbies, I feel much calmer and not stressed. I told you that I have panic attacks and feel anxious about different things. My hobbies make me feel better.

When I was younger, I had many different hobbies than I have now. I have even tried new hobbies, like making friendship bracelets. Now my hobbies have changed and that is okay because people sometimes learn new things, or their interests change.

My advice to you is that everyone should find hobbies they love to do all the time. If somebody does not have a hobby, then you should teach them one; step-by-step. Let them explore different hobbies to see which one they like better. A long time ago my hobby was learning to speak Japanese. My mom did not laugh at me or tell me that I could not learn it. She signed me up for a Japanese language program at the Japanese Canadian Culture Centre. My mom came with me, but she did not learn a lot of Japanese. Instead I learned a lot. I can now speak quite a bit of Japanese. After learning to speak Japanese, my hobby became learning to write it and guess what? I can do that now too!!! And maybe you should follow my footsteps, that way you can learn from me what it feels like to be unique and cool.

Sometimes when I am bored, I try to improve my hand-drawings or create friendship bracelets. It is good to do hobbies every day instead of just staying home and doing nothing at all. I love to practice my hand-drawing skills by drawing fan art. Improving my drawing skills have helped me become a better artist than I was before.

My message to you is to find a new hobby and stick with it. I think it would be great to get paid money to do your hobby or find a job doing your hobby. That is my dream.

Why not take a break from all your stress and focus on your hobbies? Maybe you can focus on improving your communication skills or maybe do some research on your computer tablet or on your mobile phone. If you stick with it, you will get better at your hobbies. Do not give up on your hobbies because that really is NOT an option at all.

Just keep on trying no matter what you do and focus yourself on the positiveness inside of you.... ALWAYS.

Chapter Summary POV

- o Hobbies are important!
- o All people with ASD have talents and these talents can be a hobby or even turn into a job one day.
- o Do not be afraid to try different things.

9 - My POV on Money and Math

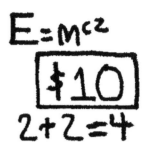

This topic stresses me out. I do not think I will ever be good at money or understanding math. Trying to manage money makes me want to give up. I know I already told you about this topic on my POV on school, but I think it is so important that it should have its own chapter! I understand how money works. When you use it to buy things, there is an amount that you need to pay with cash, credit, bank card, etc. The hard part for me is doing the math. My family, teachers and therapists have tried to teach me about money, but my brain does not get it. I do not know why. I just do not get it all. The only thing I can use for purchasing something is my debit card.

I know the names of all the coins and the values but adding and subtracting them is crazy hard to do in my head and of course I do not have enough fingers and toes to count. I have tried to use a calculator but let me tell you, standing in line with a calculator or using my phone calculator causes me a lot of anxiety. I do not want people to get upset with me or think I am dumb. I have wanted to give up many times. But I have not! My mom opened a bank account for me and gave me a card to use. I buy many things on-line and try to keep a book where I write down what I bought and how much money I have left. I tried using the excel program to manage my bank account and spending but that was even more confusing for me. Sometimes I forget to keep track of my purchases and my parents need to remind me. This is okay because I am still learning and do not need to know it well because it is not like I am going to work in a bank one day or be an accountant.

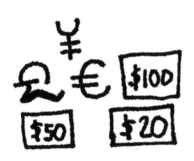

Now I know what you are thinking, "You need to keep track of your money. This skill is important because you don't want to go bankrupt." I know! I do not want to give up on learning how to manage my money. I guess this is where I need to be patient with myself. Maybe there is a program for adults with ASD that can teach me. Do you know of any? If there is not any, then someone should make one. When I was in high school, there was a class about money, and it helped me a little bit.

I still feel like money is complicated. Well for me it is. There are some questions about my spending that I am overly sensitive about and I would rather not be asked. Mainly I do not like being asked, "Why did you buy that?" or "How much does that cost?" Come to think of it; I have had different kinds of trouble with money, especially when I bought a lot of things online. Somethings can become bad because I am not particularly good with math. I have been scammed several times. Thankfully, my parents know what I buy, and they have been able to help me in these situations. Getting scammed is NOT good for me and it is unhealthy. It stresses me out and causes my anxiety to go way up. I start to HATE the part of me that does not understand and wish I were better in math. It has also made me not want to trust others. Not all people with autism have trouble with math. I am only talking about myself (my POV remember). To be technically honest, whenever I buy something online, I do not think it is a waste of money (for me) at all.

So, what can I do to get better at managing my money? I can practice every day by going to a Math website. Now that I mentioned it, yeah, it would help me out. That way I can improve my Money managing skills.

Make sense?

センスにかなってね？

(Sensu ni kanatte ne?)

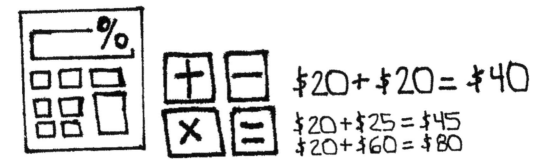

$20 + $20 = $40

$20 + $25 = $45

$20 + $60 = $80

I can also get a math book, some papers, a calculator, and a pencil. Try to remember what I learned when I was in school and practice. Maybe schools need to change how they teach people with ASD about math? Maybe they will. Who knows right?

The main thing for me is to try to think positive and do math questions every day. It might also help me to learn different computer programs. Programs like Excel can help me learning math.

Chapter Summary POV

o   Learning about money and math can be hard. It can even cause serious stress for some people (like me).

o   There are different ways to help people with money and math.

o   Practice, practice, practice!

10 – My POV on Communication

When I was diagnosed at three years old, I was not speaking at all. I eventually learned some sign language and I used a system called the Picture Exchange for Communication (PECS). My parents were told there was a 50-50 chance that I would ever be able to speak. My parents did not give up and tried a lot of things to help me and had me going to a lot of speech therapy. Who tells a parent that their child has a 50-50 chance of talking? It is like they are betting in Las Vegas. Well, guess what, they lost!

So, what helped? Using pictures really helped me a lot! My parents and therapists did not realize that on the cards with the pictures they were showing me there were words. I learned to read by learning the words on these cards. I started to use a few words and eventually put sentences together. One day my therapist was using cards to teach me the names of my family. The pictures of my family were on one side and their names on the back. She turned the cards over as a game (kind of like the Memory game) and she asked me to find different family members. Well, to her surprise I did not turn the cards over to find their picture because I was reading their names on the back. Pretty cool, huh? So, when my parents realized this, they put up labels all around the house to help me learn new words.

Over the years, it really helped me to keep my own word dictionary to learn new words and their meanings. Using the correct grammar is a lot harder (even today - remember, MICHAELISM). Sometimes, when people speak to me, I do not always understand everything they are saying. Sometimes if people talk too fast or if they use words that I am not familiar with, it is hard for me. I have learned to ask people to explain things so I can understand. It is important to teach your child to do this too. Otherwise they will not know what people are saying. For me it really helps if people are very polite, not rude, and do not use jokes. Once in a while if a person uses a joke or laughs, I think they are insulting me. So, it is better to be clear, okay.

Sometimes it is still hard for me to communicate verbally what I am thinking and feeling. I have always preferred to write or type things down. When I feel sensitive about something it helps if my therapists or family write things down for me. When I read it, it helps calm me down. I guess that is why I wanted to write this book.

Speaking of my everyday life, although I still have some communication problems, I know that I am getting better at communicating with people (outside of Social Media). I have faced many challenges over the years. I have problems with a range of verbal and nonverbal skills, grammar, using the correct pronouns and responding when I am spoken to. But, in the end, I am improving. Even writing this book has helped a lot.

My message to everyone is to never give up on teaching communication skills to others. Yes, it can be very tricky and hard for some people, especially those with autism. The thing is you must find the best way to help that person. Not every person with ASD will be able to speak. That is OKAY! You can find a different way like using an iPad, or PECS or sign language to communicate. There might even be an invention in the future. Who knows, right? The important thing is to believe in them and help them communicate.

Communications are the best.

コミュニケーション、最高。

(Communications, saikou)

Chapter Summary POV

○ Do not believe everything the doctors tell you (My POV remember. I did learn how to speak!)

○ Find a way to teach a person how to communicate that is best for them.

○ Never give up on teaching communication. It is important!

11- My POV on Volunteering

ボランティア

Volunteering is so important for people on the spectrum. I started volunteering when I was in high school. To graduate I had to do 40 hours of volunteering. The first place I volunteered was HMV (His Master's Voice), [19] and then I helped at Best Buy [7]. I think I enjoyed volunteering at HMV [19] so much because of my interest in music.

At first, I did need help at HMV. My support workers would always be close by in case I needed help. I would stack shelves, answer customer questions about music and even movies. This part was easy. Sometimes they asked me questions that I could not answer and that made me anxious. I was afraid that a shopper would get upset or annoyed with me if I could not answer their questions, and I did not want this to happen. I was also really scared that I would have to deal with money. Remember, what I said about using money. It is really complicated for me to. My worker taught me to say *"I'm not sure. Let me find someone who can help you."* Simple right? Well now I think so, too. But, in that moment, when I felt anxious it was like my brain freezing. I felt stuck. When I feel stuck, I start to have a panic attack and I only think "I can't" or "I don't know" thoughts. If someone asks too many questions or keeps talking then it only makes it worse. The good news is that I did do well at HMV [18]. In high school I also had a work placement program. This program tries to match your skills and interests with a job in your community. Great, right?! I think ALL schools should have this program for every year of high school; and is should not just be for people with autism or other needs. I mean EVERY student in high school would benefit from this program.

My next big volunteering job was in 2013. I ended up volunteering at North York General Hospital (NYGH). The reason why I chose to work at NYGH is because it was an amazing place for my father to work at. The people were so kind to me when I visited him (he is a doctor who works there) and they made me feel comfortable. Even though my father worked there, to get the position, I still had to meet with the Volunteer Coordinator and go through an interview- scary! My therapists helped me practice for the interview and work on my resume. They wrote down some sample questions and answers. This was so helpful. My mom kept this information in a binder. She loves file folders and binders. She keeps everything! This is good because I could go back and look at it to practice.

At the hospital, I started at the front desk. This was okay but at times I found it kind of hard. I sometimes needed to pace and self-talk. Some people did not understand why I needed to do this. I hope they did not think I was weird or scary, so the volunteer coordinator had to find me a different job. For example, I delivered mail, I put papers together and I even delivered flowers. (Oh, and guess what, this is the same hospital that I was born at, on July the 20th, 1991).

Volunteering helps give people with ASD a chance to practice different skills. Volunteering has been an incredibly positive experience for me. I still go every week regularly and try not to miss my shift. I am always welcomed warmly. My language and social skills have got even better because of my volunteering experience. I started to feel more comfortable and confident too. A lot of people on the spectrum do not have jobs and I think this needs to be changed. People with autism can work if you give them a chance. It can help people like me to gain experience and then also help me decide where I would like to work. It was not always easy that is for sure.

The best thing someone can do to help people with ASD is to FIRST give them a chance. Every person on the spectrum can find something they are good at doing or interested in, even if it is only to volunteer. The SECOND thing is to let them have breaks because breaks help them manage if they feel anxious. I sometimes find it helpful to have breaks.

Now as an adult I still volunteer one day a week. I have always volunteered at the same hospital. I have been volunteering there for over 6 years (since 2013) and they even gave me an award. I have done different jobs at the hospital. This was good for me. Doing the different jobs gave me a chance to practice different things and see what I prefer to do. It also helped me see what I was good at doing (and not particularly good doing). My mother always says, *"A good deed done is a Mitzvah."*

Good deeds are the best.

善行、最高。

(Zenkou, saikou)

Chapter Summary POV

- Volunteering helps people with autism in so many ways.

- Start with something they can do that is easy for them and what they enjoy doing.

- Give them a chance to try different roles so they gain lots of experience.

---

12 – My POV on Self-Stimulatory Behaviour

Do you know what self-stimulatory behaviour is? Not sure. Well it is behaviour that someone does over and over. For example, like pacing (I do), twirling hair, spinning things, rocking, biting their fingernails, and flapping their arms. My POV on self-stimulatory behaviour is that every child diagnosed with Autism Spectrum Disorder (ASD) might do self-stimulatory behaviour. I believe it is because people on the spectrum can be "sensitive" to the world around them and doing these repetitious behaviours can help soothe them. Some people call it stimming. Stimming can calm them down because it lets them focus on just one thing and takes away some of the sensory overload. Believe me, there can be a lot of sensory things. Let us take me for example, I stim a lot because it helps me calm down. Some of my stimming is tapping my fingers to the drumming beat of a song. The real reason why I do it every day is because it really helps me get into the rhythm of the music. I love music and tapping is a way for me to express that enjoyment. Another stim that I sometimes do is bite my plastic link chains because that helps me calm my anxiety down. Sometimes I pace back and forth and talk out loud too. This can happen when I am waiting and do not have anything to do. Kind of like when you are bored. Oh, and when I am on the computer, I shake my legs a lot without even realizing that I am doing it. Sometimes I shake my legs so loud that it vibrates the floor. Can you imagine? I mean, really?

The good news is that over the years my family and therapists have helped me manage my stimming so it is not a problem for me in public (like when I am volunteering, out shopping or at the movies). You might have a different POV on stimming. Some people believe that you should never let people stim and others believe you should not stop a person from stimming. Well, if that is what you think, then OKAY, that is your POV. But do not forget to ask the person with autism what it is doing for them. Many people (who do not have ASD) have A LOT of opinions on what people with ASD should or should not do. Also, please know that it is a myth that ALL people with autism flap their hands. I never did and this is true for many of my friends. Oh, and I know many people who do not have autism but stim.

What are other reasons why people with Autism stim? That is a good question. Well to be honest, it has not always been so easy to determine the real reason for stimming. There are so many different POV's on this topic. Do not believe me? Google it and you will find out. My POV is that everyone is different with unique sensory needs. I have heard some people say that they think it is because a person with autism does not have good play skills. This was sort of true for me. When I was little, I did not really know how to play that well. My therapists spent many hours teaching me how to play independently and with other kids. Some self-stimming behaviours stayed with me and I do them when I am bored or anxious, but others have stopped. I also have learned how to change some of my self-stims, so they do not look too obvious when I do them in public. I cannot explain why some are easier to control. One stim I still do is called a Spit Take. What is that you ask? It the act of suddenly spitting out liquid that one is drinking in response to hearing something funny or surprising [21]. For example, whenever I watch a funny video on the Internet, I would spit a liquid beverage all over the computer screen. But it is a long story (so **DON'T** ask about this one!). When I feel anxious or bored, I do one of my stims. If I do not do one, those feelings can actually get worse. So, to help get rid of the feelings, I JUST DO IT!

My POV is that another reason why stims happen is because people with autism are trying to feel comfortable in their environments. Stimming can help a person deal with sensory overload. I guess you really need to try and figure out why a person is self-stimming and if there is anything they can do instead.

What about harmful stimming? This includes stims that are very uncontrollable, occur excessively in inappropriate settings, and can harm a person. Harmful stimming can include hair pulling, biting, hitting oneself, hitting the head against something in a harmful way, and picking or nail biting to the point of injury. I never did any harmful stimming that I remembered until writing this book. Then I remembered that I do one thing. Sometimes I pick and bite my toenails (okay, yeah sort of gross-SORRY!). Biting your toenails can cause toe infections and this is not good for your health. Sometimes I still do this when I am super stressed. I know I should stop. Okay, I will try to stop it! I wonder what I can do instead.

The real question is: *"Are there circumstances in which I should interrupt or discourage stimming?"* The answer to that is yes (well, my POV anyway). Remember what I just said about harmful stimming? Self-injurious behaviour like when someone is banging one's head on the floor needs intervention. Dangerous stims should be stopped. However, remember not everyone on the spectrum does harmful stimming.

So, my POV on self-stimulatory behaviours is that it is a coping mechanism that can serve a variety of purposes. It really depends on the person!

Chapter Summary POV

- o Many people with autism self-stim (oh, and other people too).

- o It is okay to interrupt or stop harmful stimming.

- o Try to find ways people can self-stim in a healthy way.

13 – My POV on Death

I am sure you can imagine that this is a difficult and emotional chapter to write. I was not even sure if I wanted to include this chapter as a POV. Every time I started to write I kept thinking that I should delete this chapter. My family and therapists encouraged me to keep going, so I did!

What do I want to share with you? I want to tell you my POV on death and why it is such a difficult chapter for me. When I was six years old, my Grandpa Stan and my Uncle Douglas both died from heart attacks. They died four weeks apart! This was extremely hard for me. I was too young to understand death. Does anyone really understand death? One day, someone is in your life and then they are not.

Confusingだね?

(Confusing, right? / Confusing da ne?)

During 2003-2004, my Grandpa Daddy Mordi got sick from Leukemia. Even though I was 12 years old, my parents would not let me see him because they thought it would be too hard for me to say goodbye. When he died, I thought it was my fault, I could have saved him. Sometimes when deceased people go to heaven (that is what I believe--my POV), I would think it would be easier and less painful to just forget them. But how do you move on? I would hear people say you need to move on, but I was not sure what it really means or how to do it when I still do think about them.

During 2011, when I was in Saskatoon with my mother, my Uncle Wally was diagnosed with Pancreatic Cancer. Man, life can suck at times! In the end, I am glad that I got a chance to say goodbye to him. I was very close with him. It was like an inseparable connection.

普通のつながりがないように。

(Just like no ordinary connection / Futsu no tsunagari ga nai yo ni)

In November 2014, my other uncle, Uncle Perry, died from a heart attack. My mom was terribly upset. She was close to him. He was so young to die at the age of 53. The thing that I did not understand about death was I kept feeling like it was my fault. My first thought every time a family member died was that it was my fault. I came to realize that it was not my fault. There is nothing that I could do to save their lives and it was God's decision (again my POV). I did not have a chance to say goodbye to my Uncle Perry before his funeral in Saskatoon. Maybe if I had a chance to say good-bye, I would not blame myself in the first place. But who knows, right?

In the month of November 2017, my beloved Grandma Babu died from old age. I used to visit her a lot at a retirement home. Whenever she came to visit at my home, I would fight with her over the TV. But I would always end up letting her watch what she wanted on TV. Thinking about it makes me laugh. She was a piano expert and a dancer when she was a young girl. I felt incredibly sad because (again)

I thought it was my fault. But now I know, it was not. Why do I keep thinking this? During her funeral, I gave a wonderful speech about her and I told everyone that I loved her very much.

The hardest death for me happened in December 2017 when my beloved uncle and best friend Uncle Shoo died. This was the most difficult death for me and my family. I had a wonderful relationship with him. Why did I have a special bond with him? I will tell you. Ever since I was young, he would joke around or play with me by keeping me happy. He would take me out to the movies, the Casino and took me out for dinners. He also took me bowling with my friends and made them laugh. He was a funny man and extremely helpful. He could fix a lot of things around the house. Come to think of it, I spent a lot of time with him. He never judged me or made me feel different. Uncle Shoo was one of my best friends. I could talk to him about anything and he was always there for me. When he died, I felt like it was my fault. It took me a long time to realize that it was not. His death was the hardest for me to understand and deal with. Even writing about it makes me incredibly sad. It is like there is something missing and will always be missing. Like a black hole. It is like I do not know who he was anymore. Sometimes I want to take down his pictures, so I do not have to look at them. When I look at them, I feel happy and sad at the same time. It is so very CONFUSING. What I started to realize is that when a death happens, I blame myself because I am just so sad about the loss. I think my anxiety kicks in, and I start to think "Who is next?" I start to have other thoughts like "Will I never be able to remember them?"

I have learned that I will always remember my beloved relatives and my advice is to not to forget about them in your heart. It is **NOT** your fault so do not blame yourself. Try to remember all the good times. It takes time but the pain does go away.

None of this is your fault.

これはどれもあなたのせいじゃない。

(Kore wa dore mo anata no sei ja wanai)

So please do not blame yourself.

どうか、自分を責めないでください。

(Dou ka, Jibun wo semenaide kudasai)

So, do you understand death now? I am trying to understand it more. I think it is hard for me because of all the feelings it causes me. The emotions turn into blame. Who can I blame? I blame myself until I feel calmer. I worry about which other loved ones will die. I know that death must happen, but it is hard and painful. And the truth is: I can move on! Writing this chapter did in fact help me deal with death.

Never forget who you love. Always remember.

愛する人を決して忘れないで・・・

いつも、　覚えるよ。

(Aisuru hito wo kesshite wasurenai de...Itsumo, oboeru yo)

Chapter Summary POV

o   Death is confusing!

o   It is difficult and painful subject for many people.

o   Do not blame yourself!

---

14 – My POV on Targetism (my MICHAELISM for being targeted)

ターゲティスム

Have you ever felt bullied before? Have you ever been verbally targeted by someone at school, work, or on the Internet? Not sure?

知りたいですか？

(Do you want to know? / Shiritai desu ka?)

According to Temple Grandin, a famous person on the spectrum, *"If you fit in, life is easy. If you do not, that is when all the teasing and bullying starts. For kids on the spectrum, it can be pure hell."* [19] All types of bullying, even cyberbullying can HAPPEN to anyone. But, because people with autism want friends, want people to like them and may be confused by social interactions, it can happen to them, maybe even more than others. Why, you ask? My POV is because many people with autism do not always understand the rules of relationships, friendships, and internet safety. Sometimes they can be too trusting, and others might take advantage of this. It is just like Temple Grandin said, we want to fit in and be accepted. I guess most of us do, right?

My POV is that children may NOT always realize that they are being targeted at school. Students (with autism) might think it is bullying only if they are being physically hurt or verbally insulted. So, my POV on Targetism is about trusting.

My POV and personal experience (so please do not argue with me on this one) is that some people with autism might believe everything people tell them in person or over the internet. But it might turn out that they will be hurt, blackmailed, scammed, and manipulated by them. We can be too trusting, and sometimes people take advantage of us. Another reason why people on the spectrum can be targeted is because we may say or do things that are different from others. I think people are truly afraid of "being different." We need to help people understand that different is not bad (the reason why I am writing this book!).

What have I learned? People with autism can benefit from learning the differences between friendly behaviour and bullying behaviour. Basically, what it means to be targeted. My parents and my therapists DID teach me about bullying when I was in school, so that I would know what it was in case it happened to me. I am happy to say that I was not physically targeted, but I am quite sure I heard hurtful comments (under people's breath) in my school hallway.

本当にひどい！

(It really sucks! / Honto ni Hidoi!)

We need to teach EVERYONE that bullying is unbelievably BAD and WRONG (oh and against the law), both in person and especially online! Oh, and do not forget to teach others that they should always tell someone when it happens to them. Parents should prepare themselves to talk with their children about how they should stand up for themselves. They should also be ready to respond to their child's questions and emotions. A great website to learn about more about bullying is www.prevnet.ca (for those who live in Canada) or www.apa.org (for those of who live in the United States of America).

So, what have I learned? Protect yourself. NEVER share your personal information online. Before buying anything online, always ask your parents/ guardians or someone else you trust, like a family member. This should be the MAIN RULE! Do not believe what people say to you online. There are some people who pretend to be kind and pretend to be your friend to gain your trust, just so they can take your money or perhaps they want to meet you and then…. (you fill in the blank). They do this to take advantage of you and they might even hurt you. This could happen when you are playing an online video game, or when you are on other social media platforms. I speak from experience, so TRUST me when I say, "You don't want to become a victim." It is also important to teach people with ASD about relationships. There are many great resources to help people on the spectrum with social skills and navigating relationships. There are even videos too! My advice, start early and teach this at home and at school.

Here is my advice...

- Teach about healthy relationships and bullying awareness

- **Be careful** who you trust

- **Never share personal information online**

- **Always ask** permission **FIRST**

- Set privacy settings on the Internet. If you do not know how, then ask a professional for help

- If you think you have been targeted, then TELL someone you trust

- Encourage the use of technology in the same room as an adult

- Do not buy unless you know 100% it is not a trap (just ask someone else for their opinion)

- DON'T believe someone who says they are your friend on the Internet

You are **NOT** alone, and you have friends that can help you to stand up to the bully and it is not up to you to STOP the bullying. You **DID NOT** cause it. Instead of targeting others, why not try to get along and become friends instead? That would be the perfect way to put an end to bullying at school. Who knows! Right?

Focus on the Positiveness of you!

ポジティブに焦点を当てる!

(Positive ni shōten wo ateru!)

Chapter Summary POV

- o Many people with autism are targeted because they are "different"

- o We are all different!

- o Being targeted is NOT your fault

- o Targetism is hurtful and can be against the law.

- o Great websites are www.prevnet.ca or www.apa.org

---

15 – My POV on Relationships

Relationships can be a tricky topic. I mean there are so many different types of relationships, and this can be hard for people with autism to understand. Especially ALL the rules. But you know what? You MUST teach it, okay! Promise me you will. I mean people with autism DO want relationships. They want friends and some people want more than that. Come to think of it, why do people who DON'T have autism say people with ASD DON'T want to be social. I mean, did they ever say this to you? I know I have never said it. Maybe it is because they do not understand us!

I understand there are different types of relationships and you need to experience each one. If you want a special friend or partner, and you are having a hard time finding the perfect person of your dreams, you should know the basics first. If you go online or meet in person before your date and find out the person has autism, do not jump to conclusions, and do not run away. The question really is: can a person with autism (like me) feel the true meaning of love?

Well good question! I have always wanted a chance to fall in love with a woman of my dreams. Society might think that a person with autism cannot feel love and get married. This is due to the misconception that people with autism may have difficulty feeling or showing emotions.... I think that is unfair. To assume that just because you have difficulty understanding feelings, this means it will never happen is just not right!

Many individuals with ASD do have the same wish for intimacy and of course, companionship as the rest of the population. I have learned that social interactions are the key to helping a person with ASD find a partner. But first you must help them make and keep friends. This can be hard, but you must stick with it. Just because a person has sensory difficulties or misunderstands facial expressions or even uses the wrong language, please know they are trying, okay!

We may feel afraid too. We have fears that others will not like us or will make fun of us. If we have been bullied before, it can take a long time to teach us the proper social behaviours. Do not give up or think it is not important. You MUST teach a lot of social skills in a structured way. My family planned lots of play dates for me and I went to a lot of social groups my whole life, and these helped me. In fact, I still go to some!

Speaking of affection, people with autism (like me) can have difficulties with understanding and expressing emotions, and an emotion that is particularly confusing to some people with ASD is love. I have experienced love before and come to think of it, I do even show it on the inside and on the outside. My POV is that some people may show affections in a different way than you show it. Some people find it hard to say "I love you" or to hug someone. That does not mean they do not love you. Just be patient.

The point is: To help an adolescent with ASD to be in a relationship with a person, the most **IMPORTANT** thing is to work on their self-esteem. They need to have the confidence to approach others. They need to practice the skills with friends so they will be ready for a closer relationship and who knows, maybe even marriage (I hope!).

まあ、確かに！

(Well, true indeed! / Maa, tashika ni!)

Chapter Summary POV

- o We want friends and close relationships

- o You must teach about relationships

- o A person's confidence and self-esteem are important when it comes to building relationships

16 – My POV on Accepting My Autism

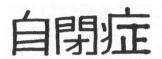 How do you accept autism? How can people with ASD accept themselves? The bigger question: How can you NOT? Sad but true, it has taken a long time for me to accept my being on the spectrum. Many times, when things in my life were hard, I would just blame my autism. I would say to my family that I hate autism or *"Having autism sucks."* I may have even said "I wish I was never born." BUT, to accept my autism, I had to learn so many things throughout my whole life. First, I had to *"come out of my shell"*. I had to know about my diagnosis and understand what it means for me. So, if you want to accept your autism then you need to learn all about it; learning first, acceptance later. The most important thing I can tell you is that everyone is different. I have lots of friends who have autism and we are ALL different. How you can you learn about people on the spectrum?

Here are some tips if you want to learn about autism:

- Hang out with people who have autism (the most helpful)

- Read books about autism (example: Temple Grandin)

- Watch TV shows/movies /documentaries about autism (remember not all characters will be true)

- Take a course (For example, Psychology)

Once I learned about autism, I realized what my talents were and of course my what my challenges are. At times, it was hard to separate what I thought was a challenge that others might have from what I thought was a challenge <u>BECAUSE</u> of my autism. In the end, I have learned it really does not matter. They are both a part of me and this understanding has helped me to better accept that autism is just one part of who I am. Right?! SO, how do you accept autism?

Here are some tips to accept your autism:

- Set goals for yourself and write them down ASAP

- Keep a journal for yourself. Write down all your talents.

- Take speech courses (if that will help you-it did for me)

- Take courses in acting/improv

- Join a Social Skills group or autism support group (I did this, and it was extremely helpful)

- Be strong!!! Believe in yourself.

- Spend time with people who care about you.

- Think 100% positive (ALWAYS!!)

- Let go of your negativity (ALWAYS!!)

- Do not give up (NEVER!!)

- Be happy being you! (ALWAYS!!)

If you have autism accept yourself for the way you are and be proud of yourself and your outstanding abilities. There is nothing wrong with being on the spectrum, you are you. You can do whatever you want as long you are NOT blaming yourself or autism. There a lot of good things in your life. Remember that you do not have to do it alone. There are a lot of people fighting for people with autism and their rights. There will be difficult days, even weeks, but never give up the fight.

The truth is you must believe in yourself no matter what you do. Giving up on accepting autism is NOT an option at all. Instead, you must be positive by standing up for yourself and for your friends and or your family.

Seek your Happiness, your Passion, your Interests, and your Road to success.

君の幸せを求めてよ、君の情熱、君の感心事 、そしてまた、 成功への道。

(Kimi no shiawase wo motomete yo, kimi no jounetsu, kimi no kanshin koto, soshite mata, seikō he no michi)

Go for it.... Do not give up until you reach for the top.

頑張れ・・・あきらめずに上へ。

(Ganbare.... Akiramezu ni ue he)

Everything is possible.... Do it.

すべてが可能ですよ・・・やる。

(Subete ga kano desu yo... Yaru.)

Do it for the world. Do it for yourself!

Autism is the best.

自閉症、最高。

(Jiheishō, saikou)

Chapter Summary POV

- o You MUST accept your autism
- o Autism is a part of you, but it is not all of you
- o Try not to blame things on your autism
- o Never give up! You are strong! You are NOT alone!

Closing Thoughts

I have autism, I cannot deny that. I want people to accept me. I cannot lie and say that I never wanted to give up on this book because I did. In fact, I wanted to many, many times, but writing the chapters in this book brought back a lot of memories. Some memories are good, and some memories are.... well they are painful. This is me and I did not choose this. This is who I am! I am proud of myself and I am **NOT** alone. I am surrounded by my family, my relatives, and my friends. It does not matter if you have a set of online friends, or real friends, or a special interest, a special talent or not, you SHOULD BE PROUD of yourself, **ALWAYS.**

When I had the idea to write this book, I shot it down in my head. Even after I started writing, I wanted to quit. I would think, *"No one is going to care about me or this book"*. I would even beg people who supported me to let me delete it. I was afraid people would make fun of me and that this book would be a huge flop. It took a lot of time and convincing from others that I really should not care what people think. I just had to do it. This book is for me! Yes, I do hope it MIGHT also help someone else who has ASD or their family members. I am glad that you are reading my book and are getting to know me, my POV's and my autism-ness.

The thing is everyone needs to try and understand more about people on the spectrum. Please try to remember that each person with ASD is so different. Surround yourself with positive people. Never give up because that is **NOT** an option at all.

What is the next chapter? To be honest, I really do not know. I know I will continue to write and share my POV's, take courses and continue to build a better me.

Live big, dream big, Seek happiness.

To everyone who supported my book. Thank you.

皆様へ、誰か僕の本を支えるよ。ありがとう。

(Minasama he, Dare ka boku no hon wo sasaeru yo. Arigatou)

Message from Michael's Parents

When Michael was first diagnosed with autism, we came across a poem called *Welcome to Holland*. This poem is about a family who had arranged a fancy family trip to Italy. Something happens during their travels and they wind up in Holland. Upon arrival, the family mentions that they do not want to be in Holland, and they want to be in Italy. After spending some time in Holland, the family realizes what a great place Holland is. For us, this common poem resonated as we had to change our beliefs about raising a child on the spectrum.

This is the story about Michael. Our perfect, beautiful, little son with Autism. He has changed everything in our lives. He has changed the way we do things. He has changed the way we have to think. He has changed the meaning of life. He has enriched our lives in so many ways. Life is never dull with Michael.

We had a large interventional behavioural team working with Michael from the time he was diagnosed. It started with the work and teachings of Dr. Ronald Leaf. Dr. Leaf started Autism Partnership and it is through this organization that we were able to start our programming for our son. We have had many great therapists over the years. This included Andrea, Janet, Paul, Samantha, Haley, and others. Michael is still under the supervision of Janet with help from Samantha. They have become Michael's sounding board. He was truly fortunate to have also had many wonderful teachers in school who have helped him.

Michael has changed our lives, we, his parents, his brother Jesse, and many others, have had to learn a whole new vocabulary of MICHAELISM. This includes sayings such as "Not too bad," "Only I can say that," "You can't talk to an autistic like that," "Dad, please" (with his hands in the air), "is this going to happen every day?" "Yelling helps me," "No, it's my way" and our favourite, "Mothers and fathers should listen to their sons."

We are truly proud of you Michael. You have grown into a wonderful young man with a unique and loving personality. Thank you for sharing your POV with us.

Love,

Mom, Dad, and Jesse

BONUS CHALLENGE: Japanese 101 (For those of who wanted to learn Japanese)

When I was young, I was fascinated by the Japanese language, so I taught myself all about it. Since then, I have become pretty fluent in Japanese. I have been improving my Japanese language skills by listening to J-Pop and by watching Japanese movies. I have decided to teach you some Japanese. Will you accept my challenge? Think you can handle it?

Ko-ni-chi-wa = Hello

O ge-n-ki dess-ka = How are you?

Ha-ru = Spring

Na-tsu = Summer

Ah-ki = Autumn

Fu-you = Winter

Ah-ri-ga-toe = Thank You

Oh-hi-yo go-zay-mass = Good morning

Sa-yo-na-ra = Goodbye

Ee-she-ga-tsoo = January

Nee-ga-tsoo = February

San-ga-tsoo = March

She-ga-tsoo = April

Go-ga-tsoo = May

Ro-koo-ga-tsoo = June

She-she-ga-tsoo = July

Ha-she-ga-tsoo = August

Koo-ga-tsoo = September

Juu-ga-tsoo = October

Juu-ee-she-ga-tsoo = November

Juu-nee-ga-tsoo = December

Nee-shee-you-be = Sunday

Geh-tsoo-you-be = Monday

Ka-you-be = Tuesday
Su-e-you-be = Wednesday
Mo-koo-you-be = Thursday
Kin-you-bee = Friday
Do-you-be = Saturday

Je-he-show = autism
Gen-je-tsoo = Reality
Shoo-je-n-ko = Protagonist
Do-she-te = Why

Me-she = Road
She-wa-say = Happiness
Ri-zu-moo = Rhythm
Oh-so-re na-she = Fearless
You-ka-n = Brave
On-ga-koo = Music
Toe-mo-da-chi = Friend
He-ka-ri = Light

Mo-no-gah-ta-re = Story
Key-moo-she = Feeling
Ko-koo-ha-koo = Confession
Shoo-say = Amends
Sha-zay = Apology
Chin-she-tsoo = Truth
Ko-wa-re = Scared
Ka-wa-ee = Cute
Oh-toe-toe = Younger brother
Nee-san = Older brother

Oh-nee-san = Older sister
E-mo-toe = Young sister

Shoo-yo-na = Principal

Soh-tsoo-g-yo = Graduation

Fuu-wa = Discord

Joe-wa = Harmony

Hey-wa = Peace

Ray-wa = Beautiful Harmony

Ah-zen-say = Safety

Teh-ki = Enemy

Ten-go-koo = Heaven

Ka-koo-meh = Revolution

Hee-mi-tsoo = Secret

Oo-key-re = Acceptance

Oh-koo-re-mo-no = Gift

Huh-Yo-she de hon no ka-she wo han-dan she-te wa na-ra-nu

= You cannot judge a book by its cover / Don't judge a book by its cover

Hi-you = Actor

Joe-you = Actress

Say-you = Japanese Voice Actor

Coi-be-tow = Lover

Ah-ka = Red

Ow = Blue

Me-do-ree = Green

Key = Yellow

Moo-ra-sa-key-no = Purple

Knee-jee = Rainbow

So na dess ka? = Is that true?

Oh-ba = Aunt

Oh-jee = Uncle

Ee-tow-ko = Cousin

Ha-ta = Flag

Oo-ta-gah-ee = Doubt

Ke-ten = Fault

Hee-nan = Blame

In-o-ree = Prayer

Yo-k-ew = Request

You-ray = Ghost

Knee-jew = 20 (Twenty)

Jew-row-koo = 16 (Sixteen)

Soo-soo-moo = Forward

Ee-ko = Onward

Na-mee = Wave

Te-ree-bee = TV

Say-show = First

Say-go = Final

Say-shoe = Last

Na-ka-baa = Halfway

Hoe-sa = Seizure

Kay-san = Disbandment

Chapter Summary POV

- o What is your challenge?
- o Give it your BEST SHOT!

Special Thanks

Kathy Tanzer

Russell Tanzer

Jesse Tanzer

Janet Arnold

Samantha Bluestein-Levy

Brett Bloski

Julie Bloski

Mandy Robinson

Josh Patten

Clerissa Patten

Michael Bloski

Rosemarie Bloski

Andrea Jacobs

Tony Everest

James Everest

Kathryn Everest

Jeffrey Wan

Haein Lee

Hailey Basest

Savanna Krahn

Turner Krahn

Easton Krahn

Lisa Kahn

Paul Kahn

Brandon Levine

Evan Mead

Shael Ian Rosen

Marilyn Rosen

Mark Rosen

Dianna Norman

Ruth Goodwin

Autism Ontario

Autism Canada

Kerry's Place

North York General Hospital

Japanese Canadian Cultural Centre (JCCC)

Finding Solutions

THIS BOOK IS DEDICATED IN LOVING MEMORY OF

Mordi Tanzer (1919-2004)

Sara Tanzer (1920-2020)

Eugene Lucille Koley (1921-2017)

Walter "Wally" Arthur Bloski (1938-2011)

Stanley A. Koley Jr. (1952-2017)

Perry Walter Bloski (1961-2014)

References

Parker, T. & Stone, M. (Creators, Writers, Voice Actors, Animators, Directors), 1997, South Park (TV), Comedy Central/South Park Digital Studios LLC [1]

MacFarlane, S. (Creator, Writer, Animator, Voice Actor), 1999, Family Guy (TV), 20th Television/Fuzzy Door Productions [2]

Groening, M. (Creator, Animator), 1989, The Simpsons (TV), 20th Television/Gracie Films [3]

Clements, R., Musker, J., 1997, Hercules (Motion Picture), Walt Disney Studios Motion Pictures/Walt Disney Animation Studios [4]

Diet Pepsi is a trademark of PepsiCo [5]

Diet Coke is a trademark of The Coca-Cola Company [6]

Best Buy is a trademark of Best Buy Co., Inc. [7]

Pokémon is owned by Nintendo/The Pokémon Company [8]

SEKAI NO OWARI appears courtesy of Virgin Music, a label of UNIVERSAL MUSIC LLC (JAPAN) [9]

NAOTO INTI RAYMI appears courtesy of UNIVERSAL SIGMA, a label of UNIVERSAL MUSIC LLC (JAPAN) [10]

EXILE appears courtesy of LDH JAPAN/rhythm zone, a label of AVEX ENTERTAINMENT INC. [11]

MISIA appears courtesy of Ariola Japan, a label of Sony Music Labels Inc. (Japan) [12]

J Soul Brothers III from EXILE TRIBE appears courtesy of LDH JAPAN/rhythm zone, a label of AVEX ENTERTAINMENT INC. [13]

m-flo appears courtesy of AVEX ENTERTAINMENT INC. [14]

KODA KUMI appears courtesy of rhythm zone, a label of AVEX ENTERTAINMENT INC. [15]

ayumi hamasaki appears courtesy of AVEX ENTERTAINMENT INC. [16]

Utada Hikaru appears courtesy of Epic Records Japan, a label of Sony Music Labels Inc. (Japan) [17]

HMV is owned by Sunrise Records and Entertainment Ltd. [18]

Quote taken from the book "The Unwritten Rules of Social Relationships" by Sean Barron and Temple Grandin [19]

Finding Solutions: http://www.findingsolutions.ca/ [20]

Definition of "Spit Take" taken from Lexico[21]

About the Author

Michael Tanzer is a young adult with autism. He is an Autism Spectrum Disorder (ASD) Advocator and has written several articles for Autism Matters Magazine (Autism Ontario). This book is based on his own personal experiences. He shares his Point of View (POV) on life with autism and hopes that the readers will gain a better understanding of individuals with ASD.

CPSIA information can be obtained
at www.ICGtesting.com
Printed in the USA
BVHW022140270920
589746BV00001B/1